Communïty

Word POWER
BOOK SERIES BY FIG FACTOR MEDIA

WordPower Book Series

For more information, contact:

Fig Factor Media, LLC | www.figfactormedia.com

Cover Design & Layout by Juan Pablo Ruiz
Printed in the United States of America

ISBN: 978-1-959989-43-1
Library of Congress Control Number: 2023915596

DEDICATION

———

To my beautiful daughter: I love you and may you experience the blessings that come with having a fierce community that encourages you to move closer towards living out your God-given purpose and aspirations.

You are my testimony on the importance of community and that anything is achievable through love, support, and faith.

ACKNOWLEDGMENTS

———

To my supportive and talented husband Jorge Guasso, thank you for encouraging me to keep going after my goals and dreams, regardless of the speed bumps. Together we can conquer it all!

To my family and friends who love me for not what I do, but for *who I am*.

To my amazing community of Latinas Rising Up In HR... words cannot describe the immense honor and pleasure it continues to be to serve you. You teach me so much as a leader and how powerful a community in action can be.

An immense shoutout of gratitude to the Fig Factor Media team—Jackie, Gaby, Kylie, Izar, Shannon and the list goes on! Your team brings to fruition amazing work and thank you for inviting me to be a part of the magix you bring to this world through writing about one my of favorite words – COMMUNITY!

INTRODUCTION:
OUR JOURNEY TOGETHER

———

Both personally and professionally I have seen first-hand how powerful having a community can be. Unfortunately, too many of us wait until we need community and miss out on the rewards of having gotten ahead of this. The search for community is meant to be a life-long journey and evolves each year as your goals change. But one thing is for sure, as you're evolving, your community should as well. In this book, as we embark on this journey together, community can also be seen as your network of trusted advisors, friends, family, board, and people of influence.

Nowadays we have so many communities for anything and everything. Especially as we look to grow towards our purpose in life and contemplate how to blend our skills and talents into who we are. I've seen the best success in achieving this by strategizing and focusing in on **who** is part of **your** community. In this book I will take you on a quick journey by sharing my keys of knowledge and success to help you get started or to re-energize your path of finding community.

To get started, when I professionally coach my clients, my purpose is to help support you in brainstorm, discovery, clarity, movement, and action. *Over the next few pages, we're going to focus on pulling back a few layers in you by inviting you to dive into why community is important, reflect on self-awareness, discover our choices, dig into passion and purpose, brainstorm on your top 5 and end with how to grow your community for mutual success.* As a bonus, enjoy the affirmations at the bottom of each page as you take the lead in manifesting a new chapter in your journey.

COM·MU·NI·TY

(kə-ˈmyü-nə-tē) [1]

noun

- A group of people living in the same place or having a particular characteristic in common.
- A shared or common quality or state
- The fact of having a quality or qualities in common; shared character, similarity; identity; unity.
- A feeling of fellowship with others, as a result of sharing common attitudes, interests, and goals.
- A group of people who share the same interests, pursuits, or occupation

I am rising up.

WHY? LIFE LESSONS

In my many years working in Corporate America supporting managers and executives at all levels in hospitality, healthcare, and technology, the most successful professionals were those that had an iron clad community around them. They built strong networks where they gave as much as they received. Over the years I chose to call them communities over networks because they provided a foundation and abundance of opportunities outside of what work could provide and brought forth development, challenges, and growth personally as well. I also learned in various studies that the effects of social interactions and being in community were so important that it could lead to living longer lives[2]. After creating a shift in my mind that my interactions were helping build a community, I noticed that the quality of my conversations went from "what do you do?" to "what inspires you or drives you?". Introductions to new people around me were done with greater intention, focus and support. Each conversation became more of a collaborative relationship driven by a mutual foundation of purpose and passion.

My desire is to invite you into my community today and share with you how to build a community of support for you, because no one obtained any kind of success alone. Over the years I continue to perfect the art of building a community around me that reflect my values, intention, and action. It's quite lifechanging to experience a supportive community that walks with you day-by-day or after years of losing touch could boomerang back into your life serving as a catapult to elevate you to the next level.

2 Source: https://uwaykw.org/how-does-having-a-strong-community-help-building-a-better-future/

I live in abundance.

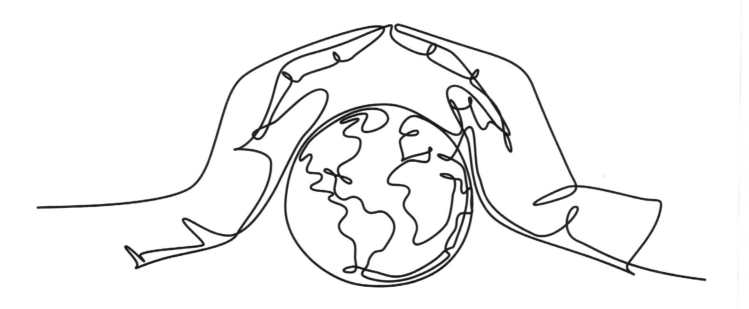

POWER OF COMMUNITY

Whether you're an introvert or an extrovert, navigating through the journey of life can have many curve balls that can throw us into different directions. It's because of those hard moments that I've grown to believe that we were engrained deep in our hearts to have community. Research also suggests that through community we can decrease the risks of heart disease, diabetes, depression, anxiety, addiction, suicidality, dementia, and early death.[3]

In my younger years I thought what helped you build community was how many people you had around you and that being extroverted was a must. The reality is *quality* is greater than quantity. It's no surprise that many of us start in school on that very quest in search of people that share similar interests: gamers, sports, music, student council, languages, culture, etc.

As we get older, becoming more complicated with our own growing interests, we search for those that share similar values, careers, and foundations. At work we search for communities to help us get ahead and get to that next level in our career.

Whichever community you decide to pursue, just know who you surround yourself with has a power to pivot your life towards or away from your dreams, goals, and aspirations. My hope is that community:

1) Inspires you to leave this world better than yesterday

2) Moves you towards becoming the leader you were always meant to be

3) Leads you on a journey, to live out boldly your purpose

[3] Source: https://www.cdc.gov/emotional-wellbeing/social-connectedness/affect-health.htm

Your Wheel of Life

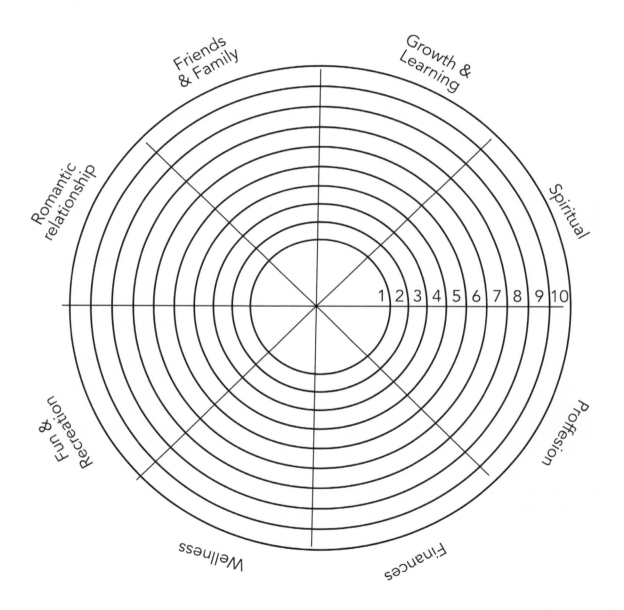

SELF-AWARENESS

Before we go looking outside at all the amazing communities there are, let's look inward first. You have all the tools and intuition on where to go next, but if you're anything like me it can get very overwhelming to just start. To begin this self-awareness, I invite you to color in from 1-10 (1-Not On My Radar, 10 – Strongly Focused On) where you are today with the following wheel of life. Be honest with yourself on how things are looking today, not where you'd like them to be or where they were. Keep in mind we're on a journey together to find community focused on progress over perfection.

The 8 pillars of community support we'll be reviewing on this wheel are:

- Financial
- Spiritual
- Wellness
- Friends and Family
- Personal Growth and Learning
- Romantic Relationship
- Fun and Recreation
- Profession: Business, Career, School

Note: *if there is a pillar missing that you'd like to focus more specifically on, feel free to add it in.*

CHOICES

At times life can feel just so difficult with all the unexpected twists and turns. However, I firmly believe that this saying remains true: *The grass is greener where you water it.*

As we continue to do the work to be self-aware of what to keep our focus on, there may be times we are bombarded with so much and can feel like things in life are happening TO us, rather than allowing them to just go THROUGH us. Sometimes we may even inadvertently choose to do nothing. It's important that as you do this work we remember that there is always a CHOICE—the choice to change our future or keep it as-is. Life is all about choices and even making the decision to DO NOTHING is a choice.

Let's take a look at your current choices by becoming self-aware of what you're working on in your wheel of life. Where do you see yourself knocking it out of the park with a 7 or more? Take a moment to reflect on that because this is where you have been focusing your energy on and where I'm sure momentum has been happening for you in that space.

Now, what area(s) are you below a 5? Life is all about choices, so let's focus here too.

In the lines below, select three areas you would you like to focus on? This is how we will begin the first steps with creating greater community and support for you based on where you are today.

Top three Wheel of Life areas to focus on:

1: _____

2: _____

3: _____

Purpose
fuels
passion

PASSION & PURPOSE

What can stop us many times in this journey of growth is that rather than focus on what brings us energy, we get pulled into doing things out of responsibility "have to do", stability "don't rock the boat" and fear "playing out all that could go wrong". Below I invite you to change your lens and challenge your mindset.

These questions will eventually help guide you towards a community that will create a monumental shift, but first let's understand what you're looking for.

Take a minute to fill in your answers to these three questions:

1. What motivates, inspires, or brings joy in your life? Why?

2. What could you talk, read, and listen to all day? Why does this light you up?

3. What top skills or strengths do you have? Something perhaps those closest to you have said? *(Hint: Look at what you scored high on in your wheel of life.)*

4. How will focusing on the 3 areas of your wheel of life change the course of your future?

YOUR TOP 5

The people you keep around you shape and influence the outcomes of your aspirations and goals in life. As you begin creating the foundation of your community, who are your top 5? Your top 5 elevate and teach you what you do not know. After reflecting on your passion and purpose, who would you think are those top 5 people that will influence your direction in a positive manner?

Below brainstorm who those individuals would be based on the 3 areas of your wheel of life you're working towards.

Include WHO you are choosing and WHY they are your top 5:

1: _____ Why: _____

2: _____ Why: _____

3: _____ Why: _____

4: _____ Why: _____

5: _____ Why: _____

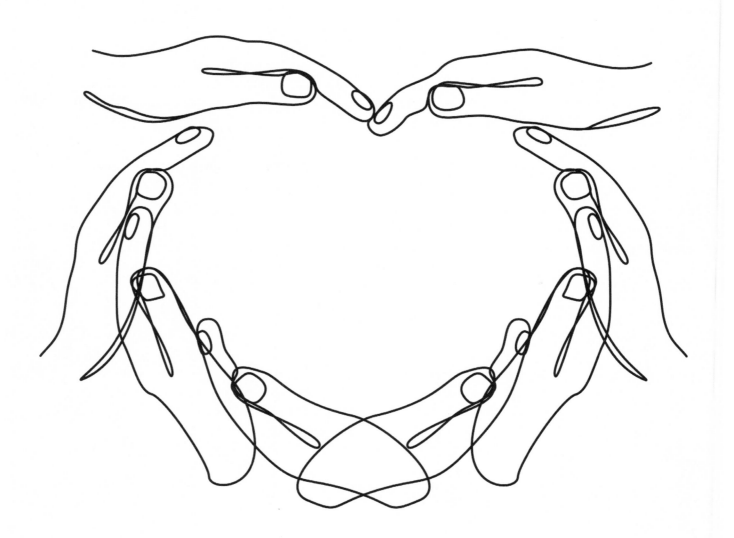

FINDING COMMUNITY

Now that you have greater self-awareness, choice, passion/purpose, and your top 5 let's talk through how to find community. Look at the themes of the work you've done so far. What communities are out there in the space that you're looking to focus on?

In each column below, place what area of your wheel of life you'll be focusing on.

Brainstorm with your top 5, your coach, friends, and family with these themes. Two, three, or four heads brainstorming are much better than one. You'll also find that most people want to support you when asked. They may know someone that could connect you to the next amazing community that could elevate you or connect you to a resource that you were unaware of.

1. Wellness	2. Finances	3. Growth & Learning
MyFitnessPal Community	Bravely	Latinas Rising Up In HR
BabyCenter Community	We All Grow Amigas in Wealth	International Coaching Federation
Search Inside Yourself	Ellevest	Lean In Circles

1:	2:	3:

As you begin to sculpt what communities to join above, in the upcoming pages you'll learn more about the different skills you may want the people in your community to have that will increase your support, knowledge and direction

BUILDING YOUR COMMUNITY

After selecting your Top 5 and joining communities already out there, now it's time to build your community. Take a step back and evaluate the skills and talents you have within you and who you have around you today. Read the definitions below and on the next page. Circle who you feel is missing around you with these skills and begin writing down the names of people that you'd like to build into your community that will support your growth:

Creative Brainstormer/Dreamer: This is who you get to ideate with no concern of judgment. You can dream of all the crazy possible solutions for the sake of just creating new ideas. This is your go-to person to build off all the what ifs of an idea. No action is needed other than to dream big together!

Challenger: This is who you go to as you test out the waters of your pitch, plan, and idea. These individuals are great to go to when trying to see what holes one could poke in your plan. They have a knack to know what questions to probe to help elevate you, your thoughts, and ideas to the next level.

Thinkers: This person is going to ask more about the data and rationale. They want to understand the facts, where your plan is going and what measurements will determine success.

Motivator: They support you not for your results, but because of just who you are. They lift your energy and spirits for whatever is coming your way.

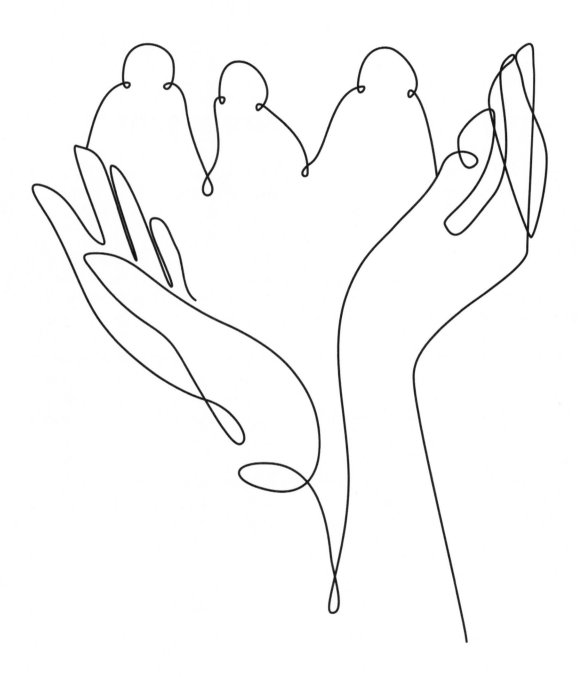

BUILDING YOUR COMMUNITY, CONT.

Decision Maker: Not sure what direction to take your plan? These decision makers are best to work with to show different paths and outcomes.

Listener: This is someone that just gives you space to speak freely. No judgement and helps you speak your thoughts and plan out loud.

Strategist/Coach: They are great to speak with to develop or create a plan to move forward. Moving from a thought to a focused action.

Sponsor: Do you have someone speaking about you when you're not in the room? This person helps elevate you in spaces you're not in, bridging exposure and opportunity.

Mentor: Someone that openly shares their own journey of learnings and success. They share openly examples of the potholes, bumps, and shortcuts they overcame for your learning & growth.

Connector: Has a vast network of people across different communities and is eager to bridge you to new contacts.

Advisor: Someone that is readily available to give advice that is targeted and more directive.

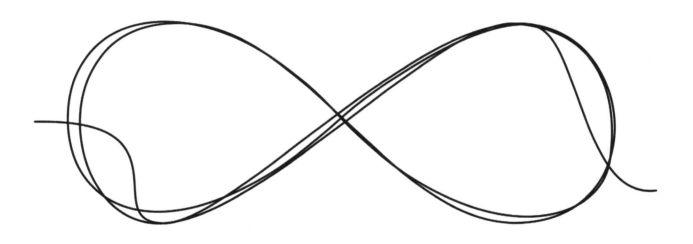

MY GROWING COMMUNITY

Congratulations, you now have a written plan for your personal community! Reflect on this list 1-2 times a year. Bring people into your circle and remove them as you see mutual value over time and aspirations.

As you work towards this journey, as with all relationships in life, keep in mind that there is also only so much that you can control. Certain people may fall short for you as they go through their own journey and may boomerang back into your life years later down the road. Focus on what is in your control and trust that the best is coming your way!

Things I Can Control:
My Surroundings
My Community
What I Say
Asking for Help
What I Eat
How I Feel
What I Think or Do
Present

Things Out of My Control:
Other people's words, opinions, feelings, actions
News
Media
Death
Past
Who forgives me
What happens around me

QUOTES ABOUT COMMUNITY TO INSPIRE YOU

A great tool as you build your community is keeping a quote close that reminds you of your personal "why". Here are some great quotes or feel free to add your own!

"I alone cannot change the world, but I can cast a stone across the waters to create many ripples."

-Mother Teresa

"The best way to find yourself is to lose yourself in the service of others."

-Mahatma Gandhi

"We must use our lives to make the world a better place to live, not just to acquire things. That is what we are put on the earth for."

-Dolores Huerta

"We cannot live only for ourselves. A thousand fibers connect us with our fellow men."

-Herman Melville

"The greatness of a community is most accurately measured by the compassionate actions of its members."

-Coretta Scott King

"Alone, we can do so little; together, we can do so much."

-Helen Kellerg

"Finding community is key for a lifetime of opportunity and impact."

-Priscilla Guasso

I am inspiration in action.

ABOUT THE AUTHOR

Priscilla Guasso is skilled at listening to what is close to your heart to get to the core of who you truly are. Many leaders find her foundational with how she radiates hope, light, and warmth serving as a reminder of positivity and one's potential.

Her two decades of HR experience expand throughout the US, Latin America, Caribbean, UK, and Canada within hospitality, healthcare, and technology.

As CEO of Manifesting Leadership Group, LLC, she thoroughly enjoys coaching leaders to reach their leadership potential, is a strong HR consultant (recruitment, talent management, DEI, culture, employee engagement, employee relations), and sought out workshop trainer in English & Spanish.

In 2020 her passion led her to become a two-time Amazon Best Selling Author in 6 categories and founder of *Latinas Rising Up In HR*™ focused on one purpose: creating a community of Latinas in HR (and allies) sharing their keys of HR knowledge and success to O-P-E-N doors of unlimited possibilities!

Priscilla proudly holds a Bachelor degree in business administration with a concentration in marketing from University of Illinois – Urbana/Champaign, Illinois. In 2023 she became a certified Executive Coach through CoachU and is working towards becoming an Associate Certified Coach (ACC) with the International Coaching Federation.

A contributing author to *Today's Inspired Leader Volume 4* and *Today's Inspired Latina Volume 9*. Priscilla was recognized in 2023 by HACE as a Mujer Maravilla recipient, in 2022 as Women of ALPFA's *Most Powerful Latinas* and 2020 as Negocios Now *Latinos 40 Under 40*. She's a proud member of: Latinas Rising Up In HR, International Coaching Federation, HRHotSeat, Society of Human Resources Management (SHRM), The Latinista, We All Grow Latina and National Hispanic Corporate Council (NHCC).

She enjoys traveling to new cities with her husband, Jorge, spending quality time with close family, and soaking up the sun in warmer climates.

HOW DOES THE WORD **COMMUNITY** EMPOWER YOU?

_____

_____

_____

_____

_____

_____

_____

_____

_____

_____

_____

_____

_____

_____

_____

I am aligned with my purpose.

Printed in the USA
CPSIA information can be obtained
at www.ICGtesting.com
LVHW080413011023
759537LV00004B/6